INSIDE A SUPPORT GROUP: HELP FOR TEENAGE CHILDREN OF ALCOHOLICS

Alateen is a support group for teenagers whose lives have been affected by an alcoholic. Alateen helps teens deal with problems caused by the alcoholic.

THE DRUG ABUSE PREVENTION LIBRARY

INSIDE A SUPPORT GROUP: HELP FOR TEENAGE CHILDREN OF ALCOHOLICS

Margi Trapani

THE ROSEN PUBLISHING GROUP, INC.

NEW YORK

Published in 1997 by the Rosen Publishing Group, Inc.
29 East 21st Street, New York, NY 10010

First Edition

Library of Congress Cataloging-in-Publication Data
Trapani, Margi.
    Inside a support group: help for teenage children of alcoholics / Margi Trapani. — 1st ed.
        p.   cm. — (The drug abuse prevention library)
    Includes bibliographical references and index.
    Summary: Explains what Alateen is and how it can help teens with alcoholic parents.
    ISBN 0-8239-2508-0
    1. Children of alcoholics—Juvenile literature.
2. Teenagers—Family relationships—Juvenile literature. [1. Alcoholism.   2. Parent and child.]
I. Title.   II. Series.
HV5132.T73   1997
362.292'3—dc21   97-4149
                                                          CIP
                                                           AC

Manufactured in the United States of America

Contents

When there is an alcoholic in the family, arguments are common occurrences. These arguments often make teens feel alone and confused.

Introduction

As Tisha walked toward her house, she was filled with dread. She had purposely stayed out late because she didn't want to face what was going on at home. "Please let it be quiet tonight; please just one night," she prayed softly. But as she opened the door, she could hear the screaming voices of her parents.

"Why do you have to drink all the time?" shouted her mother.

"Why don't you leave me alone? I'll do whatever I feel like!" yelled her father.

Tisha didn't know how much longer she could stand being at home.

Her dad usually came home from work drunk. Her mom would immediately criticize

8 | *him for drinking. Most of the time, they were too busy arguing to care about anything else.*

Tisha wished she could talk to someone, but she didn't know who to trust.

There are many teenagers with problems like Tisha's. Someone in their family or someone very close to them is an alcoholic. An alcoholic is someone who is addicted to alcohol. Alcoholics have no control over their lives; the alcohol controls them. Alcoholics stop caring about family and friends. They become undependable, distant, and even violent.

For Tisha, and the others who have to deal with an alcoholic in their lives, there is hope. There are people they can turn to for advice, help, or just to talk.

Alateen is a support group that helps teenagers whose lives have been affected by an alcoholic, whether it is a parent, relative, friend, or neighbor. However, a majority of Alateen members joined the group as the result of an alcoholic parent, and these teens are the focus of this book.

Alateen is based on the principles of Alcoholics Anonymous (AA), an organization that helps alcoholics overcome their addictions, and Al-Anon, an organization

for adults whose lives have been affected
by an alcoholic.

All three of these programs are based
on the principles of self-help and peer
support. They are rooted in the belief
that people find strength and hope from
others who are experiencing similar situa-
tions and emotions. Another important
aspect of these programs is that, by
joining them, participants each take a big
step toward changing their lives and
helping themselves.

In this book, we will explain what
Alateen is and who is involved in the
program. We will also discuss the many
negative effects alcoholism has on society.
We will look inside an Alateen meeting.
We will also discuss what it is like living
with an alcoholic and how Alateen helps
teens in this situation cope with their
problems.

This book will give you an inside look
at Alateen and show how this organization has helped many teens. This book
will guide you in deciding if Alateen can
help you.

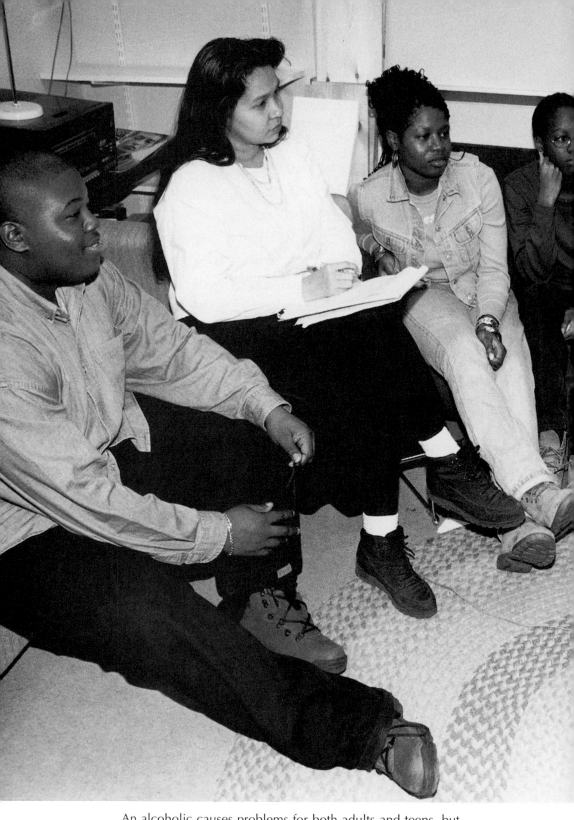

An alcoholic causes problems for both adults and teens, but
Alateen was created because people recognized the problems
faced by teens were different from those of adults.

CHAPTER 1

What Is Alateen?

Alateen was created in 1957 by a seventeen-year-old boy. His parents were in Alcoholics Anonymous (AA) and Al-Anon. That means that one of his parents was a recovering alcoholic (someone who had problems with alcohol but has given it up) in AA, and the other parent was going to Al-Anon. AA and Al-Anon are two different organizations that serve different purposes.

The purpose of AA is to help alcoholics become sober (free from the influence of alcohol) and regain control of their lives. Al-Anon, on the other hand, helps adults whose lives have been affected by an alcoholic. The group helps participants

12 | deal with the problems created by an alcoholic.

Before 1957, Al-Anon had been an organization that helped people, adults and children, deal with problems created by an alcoholic in their lives. However, teens began to realize that the problems they faced were quite different from the problems faced by adults. AA and Al-Anon recognized that teens had special needs, but it took a teen to put Alateen together.

Today, there are Alateen groups all over the world, including the United States, Canada, Africa, Australia, Europe, and South America. According to Al-Anon, there are 17,000 Al-Anon groups and 2,000 Alateen groups in the United States. Combined, there are about 30,000 Al-Anon and Alateen groups worldwide.

Everyone who has joined Alateen wants to work on changing and improving their lives. In Alateen, one of the first things members learn is that they are not respon-sible for someone else's drinking habits.

Members of the group receive support and understanding from their peers and by hearing each other's stories and sharing their experiences. By talking to and listening to others, teens learn how

Through hearing the stories of other Alateen members, teens learn how to deal with the people and problems in their lives.

to deal with their own problems and concerns.

Ages of Alateen Members

While there is no strict age limit for young people who want to join Alateen, the age of members usually ranges from twelve to eighteen years old. People who reach eighteen and still need or want a support group often join Al-Anon.

At eighteen, people often find that Al-Anon members deal with issues that are more appropriate for their age level. For example, if you are at an age where you

14 are driving and going to parties, you may have different problems from those who don't drive yet. Or if you are out of school and in the workplace, you may have to cope with things that are different from those of teens who are still in school.

In Al-Anon, members learn about ways to deal with problems that teens do not normally face.

The Teachings of Alateen

Although Alateen is meant for teens, some of its ideas come from the experiences of adults in Al-Anon and AA. Al-Anon, AA, and Alateen are twelve-step programs. All three follow the same twelve steps. This means that each person who joins Alateen agrees with and tries to live his or her life around these twelve ideas. Members try to apply the twelve steps to their relationships with other people and to their attitudes about their lives. The twelve steps are listed on pages 15 and 16.

Alateen Protects Its Members' Privacy

Like AA and Al-Anon, Alateen enforces anonymity. This means that nothing anyone says in the group, or even the fact

Twelve Steps*

1. We admitted we were powerless over alcohol—that our lives had become unmanageable.

2. Came to believe that a Power greater than ourselves could restore us to sanity.

3. Made a decision to turn our will and our lives over to the care of God <u>as we understood Him</u>.

4. Made a searching and fearless moral inventory of ourselves.

5. Admitted to God, to ourselves, and to another human being the exact nature of our wrongs.

6. Were entirely ready to have God remove all these defects of character.

7. Humbly asked Him to remove our shortcomings.

8. Made a list of all persons we had harmed and became willing to make amends to them all.

9. Made direct amends to such people wherever possible, except when to do so would injure them or others.

10. Continued to take personal inventory and when we were wrong promptly admitted it.

16

11. Sought through prayer and meditation to improve our conscious contact with God, <u>as we understood Him</u>, praying only for knowledge of His will for us and the power to carry that out.

12. Having had a spiritual awakening as the result of these steps, we tried to carry this message to alcoholics, and to practice these principles in all our affairs.

---

* The Twelve Steps are reprinted with permission of Alcoholics Anonymous World Services, Inc. Permission to reprint the Twelve Steps does not mean that AA has reviewed or approved the contents of this publication, nor that AA agrees with the views expressed herein. AA is a program of recovery from alcoholism <u>only</u>—use of the Twelve Steps in connection with programs and activities which are patterned after AA, but which address other problems, or in any other non-AA context, does not imply otherwise.

that they are in the group, can be discussed outside of the group. The identity of that person and what he or she says is completely confidential.

The reason for this is that people in the group often talk about very personal and sometimes upsetting things. They would probably not talk about these things if they thought their personal problems would become gossip or would

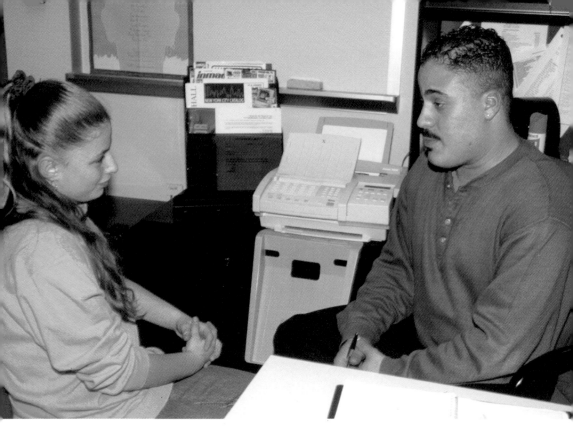

Although Alateen is a place for members to work out their problems, teens should also see a professional counselor for help in resolving other problems.

be used against them. Anyone who joins Alateen can be assured that what they say about themselves or their families in a meeting will never be repeated to anyone outside of the group.

Alateen Is Not Professional Counseling

Alateen is a place where teens can work out some of their problems, but it does not take the place of professional counseling. Alateen is just one step in the healing process. Members should also receive professional counseling. Sometimes teens

18 | who join Alateen also see a therapist or a social worker who can help them with their most serious problems, such as physical or sexual abuse.

What is important about Alateen is that it gives teens a place where they can finally speak freely about the problems caused by a loved one's addiction. Teens feel at ease talking about these problems because they know the other members in the group have similar problems and will understand.

CHAPTER 2

Understanding Alcoholism

What Is Alcoholism?

Alcoholism is a disease that not only affects alcoholics themselves, but also greatly affects their families and friends. The problems created by an alcoholic in the family can leave husbands and wives frustrated and angry. It can leave children confused, hurt, and lost.

According to Alcoholics Anonymous, alcoholics cannot control when they drink or how much they drink. Alcoholism is a progressive disease. That means that someone can start drinking just a little at a time, but eventually his or her life will revolve around alcohol.

Some people are born with a tendency toward addiction if they use drugs and alcohol. For these people, it is very easy to become addicted to alcohol.

Experts who study alcoholism believe that many people can drink moderately, or drink only on social occasions. So why are some people able to drink without becoming addicted and others are not? It is the result of genetics. Some people are born with a tendency toward addiction if they use drugs or alcohol. For these people, it is very easy to become addicted to alcohol.

According to the Children of Alcoholics Foundation in New York, there are 28 million children of alcoholics in the United States. Seven million of those are under eighteen years of age. That means that one out of every eight Americans is the child of an alcoholic. The foundation also says that children of alcoholics have a higher chance of becoming alcoholics themselves.

Alcoholism Affects Everyone

Living with an alcoholic parent can mean living in a middle-class neighborhood in the suburbs with two working parents. It can also mean living in a single-parent home in a poor, inner-city neighborhood with a parent who works only part-time or not at all. There are teens who live in wealthy neighborhoods with an alcoholic

Children of alcoholics have a tendency toward becoming alcoholics themselves.

parent who is a doctor, lawyer, or corporate executive. Alcoholism is a disease that can affect anyone.

Alcoholics and Their Families

Families of alcoholics have to deal with many problems that other families do not. Studies indicate that families with an alcoholic are often less close than other families. They are also less likely to express their feelings, and less likely to encourage independence. Families with an alcoholic parent also fight more often and are less likely to encourage their children to read or study. While all families experience some of these problems from time to time, families with alcoholics experience these problems more often and more intensely.

In many families with alcoholics, the nondrinking parent and the children are often victims of physical or emotional abuse.

The good news is that once the alcoholic in the family stops abusing alcohol, the family can function much like other families. When the family no longer has to deal with problems created by one member's addiction, it is better able to provide a healthy, safe, and

When there is an alcoholic in the family, teens are often forced to take on some of the responsibilities of the alcoholic, such as taking care of a younger sibling.

productive environment for all of its members.

Alcoholics and Their Children

Because of the problems and stress often found in families with an alcoholic, young children often develop physical problems, including headaches, tiredness, and stomachaches even though there is no physical evidence of the illness. Sometimes these children also experience nausea, bedwetting, and sleeping problems.

Along with physical problems, some

24 kids with an alcoholic parent also have

emotional problems. Some kids grow up to be adults who have trouble getting close to or trusting other people. They may be very aggressive or overly dependent on others, or suffer from low self-esteem.

Other children become very responsible, taking care of younger children in the family as well as taking care of their parents. Often these kids have trouble concentrating in school. Having to worry about whether their parents will be drunk when they get home, or whether there will be another fight, makes it hard to concentrate on schoolwork or anything else.

Problems Will Only Become Worse

For teenagers who don't get help, these problems will become worse. Children of alcoholic parents are more likely to become addicted to alcohol and other drugs. They are twice as likely as other kids to have psychiatric treatment for behavior problems, anxiety, or depression.

Some children of alcoholics have problems with lying, stealing, fighting, cutting school, and paying attention when they are in school. They are also more likely to be expelled from school or drop out

26 because they marry early, get pregnant, are institutionalized, or join the military.

With all the problems they face, it's not surprising that children of alcoholics have a higher rate of hospital admissions and illnesses compared to other young people. In fact, studies done on these young people show a relationship between alcoholic parents and adolescent suicide.

Alcoholism and Genetics

According to experts, alcoholism occurs more often in people whose parents are or were alcoholics. The susceptibility to alcohol—how easily you can become addicted to alcohol—can be passed genetically from parent to child.

However, this doesn't mean that just because your parent is an alcoholic, you will become one. Many other things contribute to someone becoming an alcoholic.

According to the National Institute on Alcohol Abuse and Alcoholism (NIAAA), while children of alcoholics are at risk for emotional, behavioral, and learning problems, many do not develop the patterns that lead them into alcoholism. Although 41 percent of the children developed serious coping problems by age eighteen, 59 percent did not develop problems.

Why Do Some Become Alcoholics but Not Others?

Why do some children of alcoholics eventually become alcoholics themselves, while others go on to live alcohol-free lives? Researchers have several ideas. They say that the children of alcoholics who do not become alcoholics themselves have several characteristics the others do not seem to have. They have positive people in their lives who pay attention to them, who are caring and supportive, and who provide good role models.

These young people are also good at communicating their feelings and their concerns to others. They are able to find and talk with someone trusting. They have a caring attitude toward others and a desire to do well. They often believe that they can find resources and people who can help them when they have a problem.

CHAPTER 3

How Alateen Helps

"*My family scene was not the greatest. My dad drank a lot, but he never appeared drunk,*" *says Amanda. "I just always felt that my family was missing something that other families seemed to have. Nobody noticed or cared about me—not my parents, my teachers, or anybody.*

"*Finally, I went to see a counselor. She told me about Alateen.*

"*At first I didn't want to go. Religion was never my thing. After all I went through, I wasn't even sure if I believed in a god. But during the meetings, nobody tried to push God down my throat. They just tried to help me cope with my problems. For the first time, I felt accepted and at peace.*"

Teens who live with an alcoholic parent often have to deal with a wide range of emotions, such as anger, resentment, and guilt about the person's drinking.

30   There are a lot of young people who have to deal with the problem of having an alcoholic parent or loved one. According to Al-Anon, one out of every five people is affected by alcoholism. Every alcoholic affects four or five other people. So that's a lot of people who, in one way or another, have to deal with anger, resentment, feelings of powerlessness, and guilt about a loved one who is an alcoholic.

Living with an Alcoholic
Teens who live with an alcoholic parent never know what to expect from day to day. They never know whether they will come home from school to a parent who is drunk, angry, or hung over.

The worry and instability most teens feel when a parent is drinking can affect their whole lives. These feelings persist at all times, not just when an alcoholic is drunk. These teens worry that there is no one they can depend on and no one who cares about them. And they also resent that they don't have the kind of family everyone else seems to have.

Most children of alcoholics feel shame and embarrassment. They are afraid to have friends visit because they never

Many teens resort to hiding alcohol to keep the alcoholic from drinking.

know how their parents will act, whether there will be fights, or whether their parents will be stumbling around the house drunk.

Along with the embarrassment and instability of living with alcoholics, many kids feel responsible and guilty. Some teens hide the liquor at home as a way to stop their parents from drinking. Others take over many of their parents' responsibilities around the house. This can mean making sure there is dinner on the table every night. Sometimes, teens even wind

32 up having to care for a younger brother or sister.

Some teens think if only they were better sons or daughters or had better grades, their parents wouldn't drink. In these families, however, the children are not the problem.

Hiding Their Feelings

One of the most difficult parts of living with an alcoholic is that instead of learning to communicate and trust others, most teens learn to hide their feelings. They believe that they are alone in their pain.

If this sounds like the kind of thing you or a friend is dealing with, there is hope. Many teens who face these problems have no one to talk to. They feel isolated and alone, but there are people who can help.

How Alateen Helps

According to Betty, an Alateen sponsor who belonged to Al-Anon and now works for the national Alateen organization, "Children of alcoholics carry a lot of guilt. They think everything that happens is their fault and if they were better children, the alcoholic would stop drinking.

"Alateen is a way to talk about feelings without any punishment, without anyone putting you down or using [what you are saying] as a weapon against you."

Alateen understands the mixed feelings teens have about their lives. The group tries to address those feelings and help teens take control of their lives. Alateen tries to teach its members the difference between the problems that they can't control and the problems that they can control.

Alateen Helps Teens Take Control

Alateen gives teens a chance to speak freely about their problems. This helps them to heal because:

- Alateen members can learn how other teens have handled similar problems.
- They receive encouragement to change from people who are trying to change as well.
- Teens are able to speak about their problems to an understanding and nonjudgmental group without having to worry about being laughed at or misunderstood.

Teens who live with an alcoholic parent often feel alone. They believe that no one understands their problem. Alateen helps these teens feel less alone by introducing them to others who share their problem.

- When teens know there are others who have the same problems, they feel less alone. This gives them hope for solving their own problems.

Detachment
One of the methods that people in Alateen learn to use is detachment. Detachment means that members learn to remove themselves emotionally from the actions of the alcoholic person. They

learn that they aren't responsible for that person. They cannot stop him or her from drinking. They also learn that they can't force that person to get help. These teens learn to stop the drinker from controlling them and their emotions.

Methods of Coping

Alateen also teaches its members that they must break the negative patterns that they have used to cope with the problems created by the alcoholic. For example, some teens had learned to cope with problems by lying to themselves and others about their problems. Others protected themselves by pushing everyone out of their lives. Others coped with their problems by doing destructive things to get attention.

Alateen tries to teach members healthier methods of coping with their problems that will allow them to take control of their lives.

Members of Alateen talk about healthier ways to: make friends; get the kind of attention and love that will be good for them; set goals and achieve them; and be responsible for themselves and their actions regardless of what others around them are doing.

Alateen members learn to set and achieve their goals.

Developing Guidelines

Through group discussions and literature, Alateen can help its members to develop guidelines for their lives. These guidelines are really ideas about how to cope with problems caused by alcoholism. These guidelines can also be applied to other areas in life.

Some possible guidelines might include learning to face problems and concerns one by one instead of ignoring problems until they become too big to handle. Another guideline could be to let frustration and anger out in healthy ways, such as exercise, instead of bottling it up. Teens

can use these guidelines when facing any |
problem in their lives.

Guidelines also encourage members to turn to people they trust for help and guidance. Members are also encouraged to use the group meetings to work through problems or concerns.

While Alateen may not have the answers to all your problems, it will help you to cope with your problems better. It may take a while for you to adjust the way you think, act, or feel.

Having someone to talk to and having a method to deal with your problems is a step out of the isolation and confusion.

Deciding to Go to Alateen

The following is a list of questions to help you decide if Alateen is the place for you.

1. Do you have a parent or loved one with a drinking problem?
2. Have you lost respect for this person and the people who put up with this person's drinking?
3. Do you have trouble concentrating on other aspects of your life, such as school, because of this person's drinking?

38

4. Do you resent doing jobs that this person should be doing?
5. Do you wish your family was more like someone else's?
6. Are you sometimes so fed up with your problems that you wish you were dead?
7. Are you afraid to invite friends over because you're afraid or ashamed of what they might see or hear?
8. Do you stay out often because you don't like the situation at home?
9. Do you feel all alone with no one to talk to?
10. Do you feel like no one understands you and what you are going through or that no one cares about you?

Most teens would say yes to some of these questions some of the time. But for teens who are close to someone with a drinking problem, many of these questions describe how they feel most days of their lives. If you feel that most of these problems are things that you experience most days, and you feel that you have to deal with all of this alone, Alateen may be a place for you to check out.

CHAPTER 4

Inside an Alateen Meeting

*A*lateen meetings happen in many places—churches, schools, community centers. Meetings last about an hour and take place once a week. Look in your local phone book or you can call Al-Anon headquarters listed in the back of this book for an Al-Anon group near you. They will be able to tell you where and when Alateen meets.

There are different types of Alateen meetings. There are open meetings and closed meetings. Open meetings are for those who are interested in learning more about Alateen or Al-Anon. Closed meetings are for those whose lives have been affected by someone's drinking.

You can find more information about Alateen meetings by
looking in your local telephone book or by calling their main
headquarters.

Sponsors

Closed meetings are informal and casual. Members sit in a circle. The meetings are run by the teens themselves with the help of an Al-Anon sponsor. A sponsor is someone who has been through the program and can answer questions and help new members adjust.

Each Alateen group has at least one adult sponsor. A sponsor does not run the group or interrupt the group's discussion. He or she is there to help if there is confusion about how to continue. The sponsor can also help if the group wants more information about Al-Anon or AA. Members can also talk individually to the sponsor if they need to speak with an understanding adult.

In some cases, sponsors are available to Alateen members by phone. If there is an emergency in the family or if the Alateen member is having a personal or emotional crisis, he or she can contact a sponsor for help.

A Typical Meeting

A member of the group who has been chosen by the participants to be the chairperson for that month will start the

42 | meeting. He or she will lead the group in what is called the "Serenity Prayer." The Serenity Prayer is a way to focus on what's important in the group. It also helps to remind members that they are not in control of an alcoholic's behavior. Then, at some meetings, people in the group may be asked to talk about what's been happening in their lives since the last meeting.

Members speak up when they want to. While everyone is encouraged to speak and share their feelings and problems, no one is forced to do so.

You will be sitting with other teens who are there for the same reasons you are. You might even know some of them from your school or neighborhood. At your first meeting, you may feel a little uncomfortable. You may want to sit and listen rather than talk. You may feel a little exposed just by being there. Or you may feel very relieved that you don't have to hide anymore. You may feel that you've finally found some people around whom you can act like yourself. You may finally feel free to talk because the other members are experiencing many of the same things that you are experiencing.

Members of Alateen are encouraged, but never forced, to speak up and share their problems during meetings.

Jennifer

According to sixteen-year-old Jennifer, whose father is a recovering alcoholic, Alateen has helped her to grow as a person. She encourages other teens with alcoholics in the family to attend at least one Alateen meeting.

"If you try Alateen and you don't like it, it's only one meeting, and it doesn't cost anything. If you want to, you can just sit back and listen. For me it was good because I didn't think I could talk to any of my friends. It was good to hear that other kids had the same problems I did.

44 You realize you're not alone out there. You don't feel as weird.

"When I first started talking about [my problems], I wondered if people would feel differently about me or my family. . . . I'm sure people think about what I'm saying, but I'm not sure they're judgmental. I don't feel judgmental. I just listen and think, wow, my life isn't so bad. There are a lot of kids with problems out there."

Speaking During a Meeting

When someone does speak at an Alateen meeting, he or she is not judged. Sometimes people who have had similar experiences will talk about how they handled the problem. Sometimes the group will comment on the story, and sometimes the group will just listen.

If there is a new person in the group, the chairperson might ask some of the regular members to tell their personal stories and explain how Alateen has helped them. This helps everyone feel more comfortable.

Alateen works by providing support and respect for every member of the group. No matter what someone says, or how he or she says it, the group listens

and offers positive and helpful responses. **45**
Members will be surrounded by others
who are going through similar experiences. Everyone in the group has commit-
ted themselves to changing their lives and
to helping their peers change their lives.

Sometimes the meetings may include
a special speaker from Al-Anon or AA,
a doctor, minister, or social worker, or
even someone from another chapter of
Alateen. Often the speakers are invited
because they have information about
problems the group has been discussing.

Trying Different Meetings

Alateen suggests that new members sit in
on several meetings before they decide if
Alateen is for them. If the first group you
go to doesn't seem to meet your needs,
try another one. Alateen suggests that you
attend meetings at some of the other
groups in your area to see where you feel
most comfortable.

Alateen members are also encouraged
to find personal sponsors. A personal
sponsor is an adult with whom you are
close, such as a teacher, aunt, uncle, or
someone who is in Al-Anon. These personal sponsors are people who are stable
and who can be there when Alateen

46 members need them. They, along with the Alateen group, form a support network that can help teens as they learn how to deal with an alcoholic parent or loved one.

CHAPTER 5

Who Are the Teens Who Go to Alateen?

*A*lateen members are like any other teenagers. They are from all races, ethnic backgrounds, and religions. They are rich, poor, middle class, honor students, dropouts, average students—they are teens like you.

According to a recent survey by Al-Anon and Alateen, 54 percent of Alateen members are under the age of fourteen. Sixty percent are female. Eighty-eight percent of Alateen members have a parent who is an alcoholic.

While kids in Alateen come from all kinds of backgrounds, they all have something in common—someone close to them is an alcoholic.

Teens who live with an alcoholic parent often end up taking care of household chores, such as cooking and cleaning, because the parent is often too drunk to do it.

They have all learned to be very careful about what they say to other people. And somehow, they have all found a place deep inside themselves to hide their feelings of anger, guilt, and resentment about the alcoholic in their lives.

"Whenever my father drank, my mother would leave the house and take me with her," says fourteen-year-old Rayshawn.

"At times, we would stay with a relative or at a motel, but never in the same place. And it wasn't for just a day or two. Sometimes we would stay away for weeks at a time. We went back when my mother was ready to forgive my father for drinking again. My dad would usually be pretty good for a while. But eventually, he would start again. Then the whole cycle would repeat itself.

"The moving around really affected me. I was so confused about my life, my parents, and myself. I resented my parents for making me live like that."

Alateen Members Had to Grow up Faster

Many of the teens in Alateen have had to grow up faster than their peers. Some of them have to be responsible for their sisters and brothers because their parents are not. Many of them don't have any

50 | supportive adults in their lives. Some kids who decide to try Alateen are afraid. They are afraid that they will do something wrong and that will cause their parents to start drinking. They are afraid that they're just not good enough to deserve a "normal" family.

They also experience feelings of guilt. Did I cause my mother or father to start drinking? If I can hide all the liquor, will my mother or father stay sober tonight? If I stay out of the way and keep quiet, will my mother or father stay sober?

"Before Alateen, I resented my mother for always getting on my dad's case about his drinking," says Carlos.

"My dad wasn't mean or anything when he drank. The fights would only start if my mom said anything. But when they did fight, it's like they were both off in a world of their own. It was usually up to me to take care of my little sister, Bethany.

"While all my friends were out partying, I usually stayed home and took care of Bethany, did all the chores, and basically did my best to hold the family together.

"I'm only sixteen. This is supposed to be my time to have fun. Why can't my parents

be more responsible and behave like other parents?"

Resenting the Nondrinking Parent

If one parent is an alcoholic and the other is not, many teens feel a lot of resentment toward the nondrinking parent. Why did my mother have to nag my father about his drinking? Why doesn't my father keep my mother from drinking? Why do I have to take care of my kid brother? Who's the parent, anyway?

The adult in the house who isn't drinking often can't manage the alcoholic and the kids. The kids often end up being in the middle or ignored.

Wanting to Escape

A lot of teens want to escape all of this. They talk about wanting to get away from everything. Some kids want to escape so desperately that they think of killing themselves. Many of the teens in Alateen have felt this way at one time or another, but many say that because of Alateen, they don't feel so alone anymore. There is hope.

One sponsor of an Alateen group says, "When teens first come to Alateen, they all share the same problems—they believe that somehow the drinking is their fault,

52 | they feel very much alone, and they've learned not to trust anyone. They had to get tough and grow up quickly because of their lives with alcoholics. Many of them just want to escape. We start by talking about how they are not to blame for the alcoholic's behavior. They need to know that it's not their fault. And we work on communication in the group. So many of them have not learned how to trust or how to talk to people. Alateen is a safe place where they can say anything they want and they will be listened to."

"I was so ashamed of my mother's drinking, my home, and my life in general," says fifteen-year-old Raina.

"I didn't want anyone at school to find out, so I kept to myself. I never talked to any of the other kids at school because I was afraid they would find out. I never invited anyone over to my home and never went to hang out with other kids.

"But when I started going to Alateen, I found a place where I didn't have to hide the truth anymore."

Teens in Alateen

Alateen is very much like any other group of kids coming together for a purpose.

While you may not like everyone in the group, all Alateen members seem to agree that the groups are not snobbish. Everyone respects each other in the group. For many, the group becomes their second family, their closest friends.

When new groups form, it sometimes takes a little while for everyone to feel comfortable. As one group sponsor explains, "Alateens (teens in Alateen) are like any other group of teenagers. Sometimes some of the people in the group are disruptive—they throw paper around or talk while others are talking. When that happens, the chairperson or sponsor may ask for feedback at the end of the meeting. [This is] so group members can discuss the disruptive behavior and what to do about it. The group may decide on some standards of behavior for their future meetings. . . . The group itself decides whether to change the standards for the meeting."

Learning Healthy Ways to Communicate

Because kids have so many complicated feelings about living with an alcoholic, discussions in Alateen meetings can be very broad. Sometimes the chairperson

54 | will pick a topic like anger, resentment, fear, or guilt, and the group will talk about how that emotion affects them. Alateens get to be pretty good at communicating their feelings and recognizing what their problems really are. They learn how to tell others what they are really thinking without being afraid of losing friends. They learn how to trust other people.

Because so many children of alcoholics have never learned what it's like to set a positive goal and reach that goal, Alateen groups will often work on those skills together. For many people, being in Alateen means learning how to set goals and standards for living. These are not easy things to do, but many Alateen members say that having the support of the group helps them to stick to the goals they have set.

Nobody Is Perfect All of the Time

One of the things that many people in Alateen and Al-Anon talk about is that no one is expected to be perfect all of the time. People will set standards and goals for themselves, but things will come up that will prevent them from always sticking to those goals. This, of course, happens to all of us at one time or another.

Alateen teaches its members healthy ways to communicate.

For the teens in Alateen, whose families might not be able to help them get back on track, the group assumes that role. These teens have learned to get the support they need from other members. They are working positively to improve their lives.

CHAPTER 6

Hope for the Future

*"**B**efore Alateen, my life was just a mess,"*
says fourteen-year-old Constance. "When my
parents divorced, my mom started drinking.
At first, it was just a couple of glasses of wine
after dinner. Gradually, though, a bottle of
wine became her dinner. When she drank, I
felt like I was the parent. I had to take care
of most of the chores. I also felt so guilty
about her drinking. I thought the divorce was
my fault and that's what drove my mom to
drink.

"Alateen has changed my life. I learned I
wasn't responsible for my mom's drinking.
I also learned that my life doesn't and
shouldn't revolve around her drinking.

"Eventually, I got my mom to attend an AA *meeting. She's better now. Hopefully our lives will get back on track soon."*

Alateen has helped many teens like Constance cope with the problems caused by alcoholics. Alateen gives teens the one thing most of them do not have: hope.

Before Alateen, many of these teens hid their pain and isolated themselves. But Alateen teaches members that the alcoholics in their lives will drink no matter what the teens do. By understanding this, teens learn to separate themselves from the alcoholics. These teens still love the alcoholics, but they will not allow the actions of other people to control their lives. Teens begin to concentrate on improving their own lives. The group provides a stable environment that these teens do not have in their homes.

Alateen may not have all the answers, but it offers a safe escape from the loneliness, anger, and fear that most of these teens have had to deal with in their lives. Alateen offers teens a supportive environment in which to begin a new life that is not controlled by alcohol.

58 | *After Alateen*

After Alateen, many teens go on to live healthy, productive lives. If they do run into problems in their adult lives, many join Al-Anon. Some go regularly to Al-Anon meetings. Others go when they're under a lot of stress or when they feel like they are sliding back into old negative patterns of behavior.

For people who have to deal with the problems created by a loved one's alcoholism, there is always a place to go if things become too tough to handle alone.

Glossary—
Explaining New Words

addiction Physical or emotional dependence on a substance, such as alcohol or other drugs.

Al-Anon A self-help recovery program whose purpose is to help the families and friends of alcoholics deal with problems caused by the alcoholic.

Alateen A fellowship of teenagers whose lives have been affected by their loved ones' drinking.

alcoholic Someone who is addicted to alcohol.

Alcoholics Anonymous (AA) A fellowship of men and women who share their experiences and problems with alcohol to help themselves and others recover from alcoholism.

alcoholism A disease in which the body becomes physically or psychologically dependent on alcohol.

anonymity Keeping identities and conversations a secret.

confidential When information is kept secret.

60 | **detachment** Separating yourself from the problems of others.

exposed Vulnerable, open for everyone to see.

progressive disease A disease, such as alcoholism, that worsens with time.

recovering alcoholic Someone who was an alcoholic but who is now living a life without alcohol.

sober Not under the influence of alcohol.

susceptibility The ease with which a person can become addicted to something, such as alcohol.

Where to Go for Help

Al-Anon Family Group Headquarters, Inc.
1600 Corporate Landing Parkway
Virginia Beach, VA 23456
(804) 563-1600
(800) 344-2666
Web sites: http://www.alanon.alateen.org or
http://www.alateen.org

The Children of Alcoholics Foundation
P.O. Box 4185
Grand Central Station
New York, NY 10163-4185
(800) 359-2623

The National Clearing House for Alcohol and
    Drug Information
P.O. Box 2345
Rockville, MD 20852
(800) 729-6686

IN CANADA

Al-Anon Information Services
P.O. Box 944
Station B
London, ONT N6A 5K1
(519) 672-7310

For Further Reading

Alateen: A Day at a Time. New York: Al-Anon Family Group Headquarters, Inc., 1983.

Alateen—Hope for Children of Alcoholics. New York: Al-Anon Family Group Headquarters, Inc., 1985.

Berger, Gilda. *Alcoholism and the Family.* Danbury, CT: Franklin Watts, 1993.

Shuker, Nancy. *Everything You Need to Know About an Alcoholic Parent.* Rev. ed. New York: The Rosen Publishing Group, 1995.

Taylor, Barbara. *Everything You Need to Know About Alcohol.* Rev. ed. New York: The Rosen Publishing Group, 1996.

Contact Alateen or Al-Anon for more reading material.

Index

About the Author

Margi Trapani is a freelance writer from New Jersey. She has worked in communications for seventeen years. For the past six years, she has directed a program that produces background briefings for the media on youth issues. These briefings combine the latest research with the voices and opinions of teenagers on the issues facing America's youth.

Photo Credit

Cover and all photos by Ira Fox.